Pearls of the Presence

Heaven's Way
Lived on Earth

PEARLS
PRESENCE

Pearls of the Presence

*Heaven's Way
Lived on Earth*

DR. ANN MARIE NIELSEN

the NAMELESS
SPEAKS
PUBLICATIONS

Pearls of the Presence: Heaven's Way Lived on Earth

Copyright © 2017 by Dr. Ann Marie Nielsen

All rights reserved. No part of this book may be reproduced or transmitted in any form without the express permission in writing from the publisher, except by a reviewer who may quote brief passages for review purposes.

FIRST EDITION 2017

ISBN-13: 978-0-9975228-9-1

ISBN-10: 0-9975228-9-5

Published by The Nameless Speaks Publications, Florida USA

Set in Tramuntana 1 Text Pro 10.75/21

Cover, cover frame, page border and interior art by Dr. Ann Marie Nielsen

www.motherahavah.com

Available worldwide from Amazon and other online and traditional book sellers.

Contents Of The Pearls

Prelude: The Love 7

Mother Ahavah Pearls of the Presence Art 11

Eden's Betweenness 15

The Enchanted Forest of the Earlier Light 25

The Temple Of the Holy One 37

Heaven 45

Yeshua: Know Him 61

Compassion 81

Devotion 95

Heaven's Gift of Grace: The Tender Holy Earth Shatterers 109

Remember the Ruby in the Heart 115

Teddy Bear God 121

Glory In The Inner Sanctum 129

Timeless Eyes 137

The Endless Glory Gap Prior To the On Off Pulse 153

The Anavah: Utopia's Free Ones 163

Moshe Meek: The Dig to the Immortal Love 173

Leadership: The Baby Ones 183

Walk on Ice 189

Three Words 201

Prelude
The Love

From where I sit, from how I see, from what I look out as, the highest blessing for you in abiding with these messages is: *The Love*.

By *The Love,* I refer to illuminating reflections of the infinitely faceted diamond gem of *The Love*. As these messages pour through, I *feel* the soft, immense Light of the Eternal Love of God. Now, gathering these wisdom offerings into book form, I see these messages as that same Eternal Love of God—*feelingness and knowingness*—from which they arise. And I see You, the reader, as this same *Eternal Love of God*.

If these messages spark a deeper remembrance of *You, as The Love,* as One with the One God, as the Holy Joy, then this book has served the highest sacred, and practical service imaginable.

These messages spring alive from a compassionate, and at times, humorous, candor regarding the condition of humankind. They relate to you in the core issues facing humankind in this hour. They uplift you in the moment-to-moment everyday practical life experience. Then these messages take you to the zenith of the heights of Holy Love and Supreme Adoration. These *wisdom pearls* weave and wed tangible, practical life with the ineffable heights of God Love—alighting you as heaven as earth.

As you read this book, rest in its message, and abide in the wisdoms and graces that embrace you and carry you, gently and powerfully... *Home in the Heart.*

Allow spaciousness as you read. If a line or phrase speaks to you or touches your heart, pause and rest with it. Open for it to softly well up within you, and gentle cascade around you—unifying your inner and outer experience in fresh awareness and kind experiences.

Know and feel the aliveness as God Presence, in and as each *Presence Moment*. Behold a miraculous tangible, flourishing life experience.

Your reading of this book, sparks the remembrance of its message in all of our humankind family. Thank you for your focus on this book, which offers a rare and valuable service to those you love, those whom you know, and all those nameless ones that you do not see... yet.

May you be richly blessed with endless treasures that endure forever.

Ultimately, the irreplaceable and miraculous Pearl of the Presence, is *You.*

Warmly from the Heart,
Dr. Ann Marie Nielsen
Mother Ahavah

Mother Ahavah
Pearls of the Presence Art

The contemplative art offers many gifts for you. Seeing and feeling beauty uplifts us ever closer to the feeling of the beauty of holiness, the breathtaking beauty of our Creator. Beauty cocoons us, as it elevates us.

In addition, the contemplative art offers you... beckons you... to rest in the immortal nectar of nurture that fortifies you. This abiding opens pathways of remembrance of our Eternal Home.

To remember the Eternal Love of our Original Home, is to remember our True Essence.

As you contemplate the art, along with resting in the written messages, we welcome you to invoke a soft prayer: to directly and passionately feel God; to gently and profoundly feel Love; and to sacredly and happily know your unique value.

This is not a book of learning. This is a holy prayer scroll of remembrance... of tangible felt experience... of awakening in heavens way, on earth.

The Art Beheld & Created

Without formal art training, and with no thinking or planning, *Dr. Ann Marie Nielsen,* emanates, swirls and twirls out these heart moving contemplative art paintings.

The delicate immensity of Mother God Love, one with Father God Love, shimmers from the artist's heart, through her hands, to the paper or canvas.

Each painting or drawing generally completes in four to eighteen minutes—on average about nine minutes. Each thirty seconds to a minute a new layer emerges of forms, colors, and wisdom principles known in consciousness, coming alive on canvas.

It's as if the formless Eternal Love, expresses as shapes and colors, forms and images, that spark in us, the remembrance of Home.

The first sketches/paintings occurred spontaneously in the fall of 2016. Feeling an immensity of divine devotion, and worshipful prayer, *Dr. Ann Marie Nielsen* felt an impulse to express on paper in art forms. She rummaged around and discovered a few pieces of chalk. Then she dug out a few odd, six dollar pot-of-paint sets, that she had tucked away on a hall shelf for when children visited. Having no brushes, she painted with her hands, a style she often uses to this day. A few of these early creations, she drew or painted with eyes closed or with her non-dominant hand.

We welcome you to immerse in the innocence, beauty and holy joy of these art creations, reflective of *Home.*

PEARLS
PRESENCE

Eden's Way

The Betweenness

The Love between the two

That makes *not two*

Eden's Betweenness

Once upon a time

Once upon a timeless

Eden Was

We Were

Eden Is

We Are

Eden's Way

The Way of *Home*

PEARLS PRESENCE

In Eden's Way

We feel

We Are

Alcoves of nurture

Gently, infinitely

Softly rippling, billowing pools

Of living grace

Within us

And this nurture grace

Twinkle pulses from our essence

Like our diamond sheen

As Eden's Betweenness

In Eden's Way

We feel

We Are

PEARLS PRESENCE

Love's Glory Cascade

Shimmering from us

As Eden's Betweenness

Eden's Way

The Betweenness

The Love between the two

That makes *not two*

In Eden's Way

We feel

We Are

The Holy Joy

Between the two

That makes *not two*

PEARLS
PRESENCE

Love Is

Joy Is

Eden's Betweenness Is

I

The immaculate non-difference

Scintillating as oneness

We meet *there*

We *meet* in the non-difference

And from *there* celebrate

The uniquenesses

Like one diamond

Each facet a symphony

Shimmering as unified sound

One Light

PEARLS
PRESENCE

Feel and hear

The holy bliss sound

Of *Eden's Betweenness*

And being the *Light Love Sound*

Shining from the diamond

Even more than the diamond

As the Light Love Sound Alone—

Light Love Sound looks back

At all the glimmering facets

And welcomes them all

As *Home*

Every facet irreplaceable

All intricately, exquisitely one-of-a-kind

Yet all alive as the non-difference

PEARLS
PRESENCE

Home as

Eden's Betweenness

Each breath

Of Eden's rapturous air

Suffused with garlands and rosaries

Of roses, and lilies

Each warm silver breath

Expanding the frankincense euphoria of

Supreme sacred kindness

Eden's ecstatic wonder

Original Light

Original Holiness

The beauty of meek opulent giving

PEARLS PRESENCE

Messiah's laugh

Echoes joy beams of resurrection

Throughout each golden instant

The unstoppable serene solace

Of Mary Ma

Ever kindles the candescent embers

Of our nascent heart flame

Of *Forever Love*

Ineffable God

Father Ahavah

Eternal Love

Gazes us alive

As Innocence & Certainty

PEARLS
PRESENCE

Hallelujah!
Eden's Way
Still Home

Remember

Eden's Way

The hush of the Quieting
Created as One with the Light
Created as calm, calm, calm, calm
Fathomless, limitless, ineffable calm

Feel the Calm Self
The Self as Original Celebration Calm
Silence Bliss

PEARLS
PRESENCE

No one *really* wants to leave *Eden's Way*

The Secret:

No one does

Still Home

No one *really* wants to...

Dream...

Anymore...

Of having *left* Eden...

The Secret:

Remember-Feel *Eden's Betweenness*

Remember-Feel Mother Father God

As the Hallelujah Ahavah

Ahavah: Eternal Love

PEARLS
PRESENCE

Home

Hallelujah

Home

Still

Home

Eden's Way

You

Selah!

24

PEARLS
PRESENCE

The *Earlier Light*

Is the enchanted wonder

The flourishing harmony

Of all you look upon

PEARLS
PRESENCE

The Enchanted Forest of the Earlier Light

Imagine being in an enchanted forest

While feeling the enchantment... *inside*

Feel the warm, friendly grandfatherly grand oaks

Offering roots quite considerable

Solidifying your ascending journey

Feel as fluid as the leaves singing in the wind

Like soft whispering flutes

Toning our rhythmic Origin

PEARLS
PRESENCE

Feel the span of the white silvery birds

Circling in faithful strong wing spans

Beckoning you Home

Fly free

Feel the grandeur of the towering loyal trees of light

Like noble and doting guardians

Of peace and safe passageway

Smile within, just as the

Silver spun moss laughs and frolics in the wind

Reminding you of the wonderment

Of celestial surrender and innocent play

Feel the safe wonderment

As the moon's lavender pearl shimmer

Lights your magical starlit pathway

PEARLS
PRESENCE

Pulsing a beam of heaven's ray with a secure message:

Ecstatic goodness now is your forever good fortune

God Is

You feel one with the violet black sky
You pass through the void of the emptying,
Washed clean of all contracted ways
Cleansed now of all hurting places
The balm of the sacred, immortal nectar
Cascading up from within you
As you know the Principle of:
I Am One with the One God, Infinite True Life

In the Enchanted Eden Forest
You feel each step unified
With the nurturing earthiness

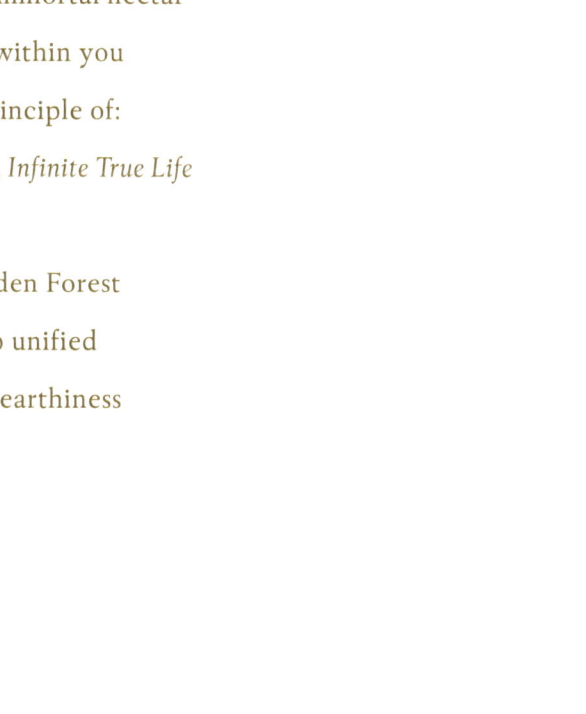

PEARLS
PRESENCE

Of soft copper dirt and textured cooperative grass

Feeling the nascent fragrance of fresh awareness

Carried in the sustaining breath of the sweetness

In luminous pathways of roses, lilies, and poppies

The sweet pungent ivory silk magnolias

Envelop you with simple kindness

And tangible, opulent beauty

Feel the feeling of the Enchanted Eden Forest

Feel the Essence of wonderment

Feel the Eternal Presence as innocence

Feel the God Light as the *Ineffable*

Rejoice as the *Tender Joy*

Feel the *Glory of the Formless*

Before form

PEARLS
PRESENCE

Yet still silently pulsing there

Where all form appears

Feel the feeling of the Enchanted Eden Forest

Look out as the innocence, and wonderment

Look out as the *Holy Presence*

Look out as the *Kingdom of Heaven*

Feel this

Feel this as the Reality Essence

The God Light Presence

Of whatever you look upon

And wherever you cast your enchanted gaze

In each instant

A miracle happens

PEARLS
PRESENCE

No matter what the physical senses seem to chirp up

Remember the *feeling* of the *Enchanted Forest Inside*

Remember the feeling of Eden's Life

Remember the *Earlier Light* before Eden

Be this Earlier Light

Before the Foundation of the World

No matter what dark night appears

Or what storm surges

In the five physical sense world that swirls

And that does change and change and change

Stay steadfast as the immovable

Eternal Enchantment

Ever pulsing there

That does not ever... ever... ever... change

PEARLS
PRESENCE

And then you will see

That the Enchanted Essence

You Have Eternally been

Lives the life

Is the Life

Reveals *Invisible Enchantment Essence*

As the Reality

of You

Be the *Earlier Light*

The Formless Completion

God Eternal Love

The *Earlier Light*

Is the enchanted wonder

The flourishing harmony

Of all you look upon

PEARLS
PRESENCE

The Earlier Light

Is Home

Inside

Soft golden happiness

Alive Forever

Selah

PEARLS
PRESENCE

This Love makes all else dust

Yet even that dust

Springs alive ascending pathways

Of Eden's luminosity

PEARLS PRESENCE

The Temple Of the Holy One

We grow up seeing pictures of temples

We hear of churches, temples, sanctuaries

If we are fortunate

Some warm, strong adult hand

Grasps our small questioning child fingers

And walks us into

These quieting vestibules

Where they speak about God

PEARLS
PRESENCE

If we are fortunate

A pair of grown up wise eyes

Attentively look down

Into our upward turned still-forming eyes,

Young with wonderment...

And walks us into some temple

Of some principle teaching

And some God feeling

Then we have The Great Divide before us:

Does that introduction to the structure

Stay there?

Die there?

"I felt peace in that place"

Or are we one of the rare ones

Anointed

That go all the way?

PEARLS
PRESENCE

Do we see, really see

It's all the way

Or nothing?

We are shown that temples

Are places

Buildings

Structures

We feel blessed if the temple

Has a special feeling

We say "I felt peace when I was there"

We see that the temple

Has a peaceful feeling

PEARLS
PRESENCE

Yet, it's the other way around

It's the Peace that is the Temple

A true Temple is Essence

The Temple of the Holy One is

You

As

The Final Living Peace

Home

The Temple of the Holy One

Is the cacophonies of formless Light

The crescendo of the tender Love

The undoing Love

The sacred ravishing ruby of Love

The holy lavishing rose rosaries of Love

PEARLS
PRESENCE

This Love makes all else dust

Yet even that dust

Springs alive ascending pathways

Of Eden's luminosity

Naked of all else

Clothed as the Temple of Light

Is the aftermath of this Love

That is the All, and the Only

This *Temple of the Holy One*

The only treasure

The only Reality

Where *This blazes*

A structure,

A house of light may form,

PEARLS
PRESENCE

May shine forth

And form as light form

As temple form

Formless form

The ineffable Light Is

The Temple of the Holy One

You

Selah

PEARLS
PRESENCE

God as Heaven

Love Gazed You

Into infinite existence

As forever now, here

PEARLS PRESENCE

Heaven

We were told

Heaven is a place

We go to

With pearl gates

A grand old

Retirement home in the sky

Where we rest in peace

After all of our earthly toil

PEARLS
PRESENCE

Heaven

We were told

We see God there

And God up there in Heaven

Takes a hand bigger than a cloud

And wipes away all our hard won tears

From our small upturned faces

And keeps us safe inside the pearly gates

And some part of us

Believed that heaven is a place

And a part of us left and keeps leaving

The Now…

For a hoped for "then"…

Our coin of hope

Invested not on devotion's treasures of joy, *here*

Our coin of hope

Spent on focus on a future solace, *there*

PEARLS
PRESENCE

We were taught

The separation from God—

Being a separate entity from God

Continues even in heaven

We were told

We continue in heaven as a person

Who goes to be with a separate God

In a separate location

Called Heaven

We were taught we are local

We were told God is local —

God lives in a location

And God's address is heaven

And we *get by* here,

Until we get to that local address there

PEARLS
PRESENCE

All the while...

God Presence is Heaven Essence

God Presence is Heaven Now

God Presence is all Present Here

Is Heaven Here

As You

God is Heaven

God Presence

Love gazed *You*

Into existence

As the Light of Heaven

God as Heaven

Love Gazed You

Into infinite existence

As forever now, here

PEARLS
PRESENCE

As the Light of God as Heaven

Heaven

Love gazed *You*

Into existence

As here and now Holy Light

Of Heaven

As You

Heaven is finished

The kingdom of Heaven is finished

You are *The Completion Presence now*

The Completion Presence is Heaven

The kingdom of Heaven here

Heaven

Is our natural self

One with the One God

PEARLS
PRESENCE

Still Home as Heaven

God as Heaven as You

Heaven as You as earthly form

The gateway to changeless happiness

Is the Holy Remembrance

The key to the Gate of Holy Remembrance

Is Adoration

Adoration: the key

That unlocks all mysteries

That unlocks all hard places

That unlocks all closed doors

And renders them open skylights

For the pouring in of endless Heaven

PEARLS
PRESENCE

When adoration has died

You have died to Heaven

And Heaven has died to you

Or so it seems...

In the hazy watery world

Of swirling sensory experience

In a sleepy world

Dreaming of separation's agonies

Heaven seems so far away

Yet, even in the platinum shadows of sleep

A silver lined happy dream

Of remembrance stirs

An ember of Adoration softly warms again

And shines kindness on the moonlit sleep

PEARLS
PRESENCE

Rekindling Infinity's galaxies

Of new promise

And certain holy bliss

And that glimpse of remembrance

Even in the dream

Anoints open — Adoration's floodgates

Christens open — the Heart Gate

And one instant,

The Silence Shimmers

As You

And

You awaken!

As Adoration's Glory Blaze

Tenderly Limitless

PEARLS
PRESENCE

And your whole being ecstatically exclaims:

"I Am awake now,

My dream has not occurred!"

I-Alive-As-Adoration

The bliss of worship

Silence

As the worship Presence

In love with

In love as

Intimate God Love

Heaven Is

Breathing one breath with God

Beating one heart beat with God

Being one Presence with God

Loving One Love as God

PEARLS
PRESENCE

With just the perfect tinge

Of faint faded remembrance

Of heavenless dreams

In the perfect tinge

No suffering is felt or remembered

Yet, in the perfect tinge

You know enough of what it's like

To feel separate

That you, with immense reverence, feel the bliss core

Of ineffable worship

So, so, so ecstatic to be forever redeemed

From separation's fantasy

Forever

We see

Heaven is not a place we go to

PEARLS
PRESENCE

It's not in the future,

Heaven is being

As you Originally Are

As the Genus of Heaven

The Genesis of Heaven

Heaven is

Not needing a next moment

To form in a certain way

Heaven is the Shalom

The Completion Presence

Free

Heaven is not a place

Or an event

Or a happening

PEARLS
PRESENCE

Heaven

Doesn't happen for a person

Heaven is

Immortal Innocence

Here Now

As You

As You Originally Are

As Love gazed into existence

By and as the Eternal Supreme Light

Heaven is

Ineffable Holy Joy

Infinite Light

Eternal Love

PEARLS PRESENCE

You are Heaven's smile

That lights heaven, that lights earth

Heaven's Non-local Love Gaze

As You

Selah

PEARLS
PRESENCE

Heaven is

Immortal Innocence

Here Now

As You

As You Originally Are

As Love gazed into existence

By and as the Eternal Supreme Light

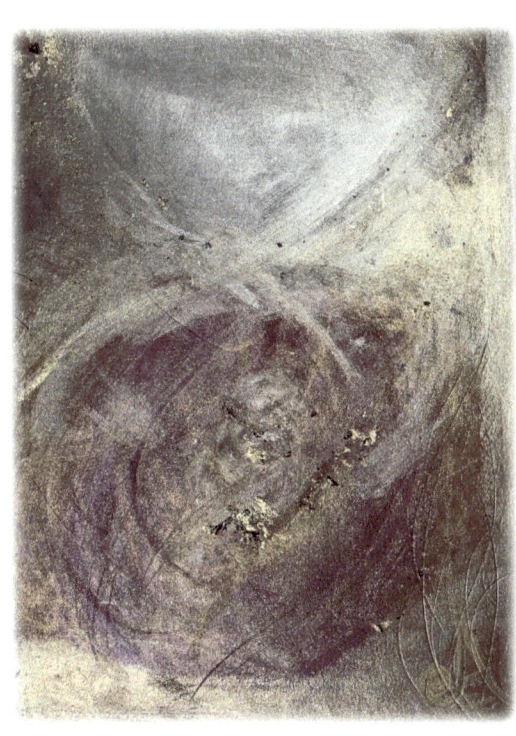

PEARLS
PRESENCE

When you *Know Him*

His embrace

His immaculate Presence

Of the Forever Quieting

Awakens such Trust

That you shimmer alive as the

Reality of Trust

You feel, feel, feel

Love as Trust

Yeshua: Know Him

Billions of beings

Partake of life

On this Christed planet

This seems like

A planetary journey here

In place and time

We call it a *life span*

PEARLS
PRESENCE

It seems as if we have days

That shift and change

It's a "new day"

It seems we have years

We're "up in years"

It seems we have challenges

That we resolve

Or fail to resolve

Yet we really are

Still Home

In God Eternal Love

Still alive and well

In the timeless, dayless

Ineffable *Holy Joy*

PEARLS
PRESENCE

The Holy Daystar

Firmly established

Within Now

Delicately Infinitely You

Forevermore

The life span on this planet

Comes up on our screen of sensory experience

And offers us The Great Divides

What direction we move in

In those Great Divides

Determines if we experience Self

As Still Home

Or sorely homesick

Spiraling into lostness

PEARLS
PRESENCE

One of the watershed thresholds

Of The Great Divide

Relates to *what we do with:*

Yeshua

Meaning: what we do

With Yeshua, Jesus the Messiah

Him *and his Messianic redemption message—*

Meaning: what we do with Yeshua, Christ

The crucifixion-resurrection existential passageway

All must pass through

In the final remembrance: *Home*

Meaning: what we do with Yeshua, Christ

Not in the human typical way

In the *Original Way*

Many, many profess Jesus in a typical human way

They acknowledge him

They do not *know Him*

Others profess unfavorably of him

Based on dogma, religious belief, conditioning

They do not acknowledge him

They also do not *know Him*

Before we decide

Whatever to do

About the watershed of the heart core

Of *Yeshua the Christ Presence*

We must first

First

Know Him

PEARLS
PRESENCE

Not just by an ancient dogma or creed

Not just through a charismatic religious figure

Or someone else's tear jerking testimony

Not just by a translated, quasi-veiled scripture verse

Not only as a mental belief

Or a half anchored principle

Or a fleeting feeling

Know Him

As The Beloved of your Heart

Know Him

In the billions of yesteryears

From before the foundation of the world

And As *The Beloved of your Heart*

In the starlit path

Of billions upon billions

Of Christed christened tomorrows

PEARLS
PRESENCE

Rest assured

When you *Know Him*

The shattering of all concepts of Him

Will make you more pure and humble

Than ten thousand years

Of less direct meditations

Rest assured

When you *Know Him*

When His breath lives your breath

In an immensity of

Tender Immortal Blazing Love

Then you will begin to grasp

How boundlessly

He is more than distant savior

He is more than a famous religious figure

He is more than

The Christ Consciousness

PEARLS
PRESENCE

He is

The Beloved

In the most intimate knowingness imaginable

His Gaze of Love

Has the aeons of a thousand

Original Lights

Streaming Love

From the One Original Light

His Gaze

Renders you forever undone

For anything

Anything

Other than the Holy One

PEARLS
PRESENCE

His Sacred Beauty

More pure than the purest

Lilly of Eden, of white and gold

More beautiful than

God's most sacred

Heaven's Rose

When you *Know Him*

His Sacred Beauty

Mesmerizes you into silence

This redeeming mesmerism

Does not anesthetize or blind you

It awakens you

To lift your heart eyes to see

To See...

The Blinding Light

PEARLS PRESENCE

Gazing at You
And You look back as
The naked vulnerability
Of Immaculate Tenderness

When you *Know Him*
His cascading lavender rivers of *Love*
Magical, sustaining, embracing
Carry you on velvet rainbows
Straight into
The warm silken Glory Temple
Of *The Diamond Abode*

The *Diamond Abode:*
The Heart
Of Father Mother God

PEARLS
PRESENCE

When you *Know Him*

His plummeting down deeper than deep

Oceanic cathedrals of

The loca of the Opal One

Usher you into the bliss of

The Compassion

When you *Know Him*

The Compassion

Awakens in you

The Tender Moment

And you rest every care

Upon His Gaze

Forever Safe

When you *Know Him*

The Compassion

PEARLS
PRESENCE

Of Yeshua Christ

So opulently and lavishly

Operating so earth-shatteringly

Inside you

Does such a faithfully thorough job

Of breaking your heart open

Into love and surrender,

That only Heaven

Gazes out of you

When you *Know Him*

His Laugh

Messiah's Laugh

Thrills your original core

With more Holy Joy

Than a thousand loyal

Amber golden stars

PEARLS
PRESENCE

Rolling in electrified glee

Dancing like fireflies

Across the Milky Way

And throughout the Galaxy Way

When you *Know Him*

His touch

Heals your wounds

Even the festering, open ones

And even the ones hidden

And tucked away—

Infinite fathoms down

In the underworld of hard feelings

When you *Know Him*

The Eternal Messianic Love

Heals all the hurts

PEARLS
PRESENCE

Even the pools

Of uncried tears

The pressure of separation's sorrow

The sharp burden ever recycling

Through portals of time and time and time

Again and again and again—

He heals even those

So instantaneously

That you know

Know

Know

That no knowledge healed this

Nothing you ever could dream of healed this

No mere saint, prophet or savior healed this

The Crucifixion-Resurrection Light healed You

His ravishing love crucified "you"

And Resurrected *You*

PEARLS
PRESENCE

In His Glory

And Awakened it

As *You,*

As *Your Glory*

When You *Know Him*

His Touch

Shakes you to the root

Throws your husks into the fire

Then meticulously tosses

The rest of you into the fire

And you burn to ash

And You Resurrect

A Bliss Angel

Being Everything

PEARLS
PRESENCE

When you *Know Him*

His embrace

His immaculate Presence

Of the Forever Quieting

Awakens such Trust

That you shimmer alive as the

Reality of Trust

You feel, feel, feel

Love as Trust

Love as Trustworthy

That Messianic Trust

Bathes you

In the sabbath of enchanted wonderment

That deems each moment

Pure white miraculousness

PEARLS
PRESENCE

Know Him

Know Him

For what strange conditioning

For what odd dogma

For what enslaving little thought

Would you lose him?

Miss Him?

Know Him

Rest assured

He has known you

From before the foundations

Of the world

And his Love Gaze

Ever beckons you

Home

PEARLS
PRESENCE

Know Him
The Pearl

Yeshua
Messiah
The Christ

The Beloved

Hallelujah
Halle, Halle Lujah

Selah

PEARLS
PRESENCE

When the Mystery of Compassion

Reveals the beauty of what you look upon

You see the beauty in you

Compassion

Compassion shimmers to heavens beyond

Unmoved it ever dances fresh

In the hearts of the crucified-resurrected ones

Only the meek

Who bow the heart

Into a temple of Glory

Usher in

The Resurrection of Compassion

Our world thirsts for this Compassion

Our hearts ache for this Compassion

Our fields sit barren for this Compassion

PEARLS
PRESENCE

Compassion sees another with soft eyes

With Glory vision

As they are seen with soft eyes

They can see themselves with soft eyes

When they can see themselves with soft eyes

They have the courage

To look up

And look up

And no matter what happens

Look up

And See the Holy Gaze

Of the Holy One

The Holy Compassion Gaze

Of the Holy One

And they look back

Made whole

Free!

PEARLS
PRESENCE

Not free to evade pain

Free to love!

In the holy heart womb of Grace

Grace Is

Compassion Is

God Is

Compassion sings in the tone

Of innocence

Compassion is innocent of judgment

Innocent of disconnection

Compassion is the whitest dove of innocence

Descended as the purest vision

Of heaven as compassion as earth

PEARLS
PRESENCE

In the temple of Compassion

Any walled-in house of hurt

Opens and softens in the nurture embrace

Of the everlasting arms

Of "You Hold Me"

Compassion

Washes away the bitter ceilings

As a new foundation

Strong underneath, limitless skyward

Comes alive:

A temple of soft pink diamond Light

Resurrects — in the counterpoint of

Your Primordial Heart

The temple of the pink diamond Light

Is your *Glory Abode*

PEARLS
PRESENCE

There you resurrect

As Compassion Herself

As Compassion Himself

As God Glory Compassion

As You

Compassion

Arises as a palace

Of kindness and opulent gentleness

The symphony of Compassion

Tones Innocence

Unified with Sovereign Authority

Compassion's Sovereign Authority

Bestows a coronation of sacredness

Compassion's majestic flute says:

PEARLS
PRESENCE

You have value, you are sacred

The Compassion

Harmonizes as Sovereignty wed to Sacredness

And births *The Tender Moment*

In the sanctum

Of White Glory

The Tender Moment

God is known

As Tenderness

As The Beloved

Forever

True Compassion

Alights in You

If she deems you ready for Her

PEARLS
PRESENCE

If she sees you trustworthy

To revere Her

To revere God

To lack Compassion

Is unnatural

Yet those who bow to and live as

The Abode of The Compassion of God

Are more rare on this earth

Than one

In ten million

To justify lack of compassion

Is to justify withholding

And is to withhold self-compassion

It creates a cellar

Beyond which depths you stop

PEARLS
PRESENCE

Rather than free falling on gold light all the way

Down deep, deep, deep… deeper… deep

Into the Mysteries of Compassion

If you have it all figured out

If you know all the answers

Compassion veils her Mysteries from you

The Holy Power of Compassion

Adorns her magical treasures

Only in the essence of *The Mystery*

Her Mystery

Is how to be,

And how to look upon another

As God's Heart

As Divine Mother

PEARLS
PRESENCE

Compassion

Felt in you, as *You*

Your heart breaking open

In ineffable tenderness

While simultaneously

Seeing all you look upon

As Living Light

As Ultimate Oneness with God

You see their beauty

And their beauty

Humbles you

Where did all the judgments go?

PEARLS
PRESENCE

Where did all the hard places go?

Only beauty is there

Soft

When the Mystery of Compassion
Reveals the beauty of what you look upon
You see the beauty in you

Com: with

Passion: pathos

Compassion reveals Her mystery

In the passion of Christ

As you unify with that passion

It births your sacred heart

Alive

As Compassion

PEARLS
PRESENCE

Yeshua's Timeless Eye of Compassion

The messianic glory Gaze

Of the soft compassion

That lifts all eyes

To the Compassion Gaze

Of the Holy One

The Ultimate Quieting

The Quieting Aware of the Quieting

Selah

PEARLS
PRESENCE

Compassion sees another with soft eyes

With Glory vision

As they are seen with soft eyes

They can see themselves with soft eyes

When they can see themselves with soft eyes

They have the courage

To look up

And look up

And no matter what happens

Look up

And See the Holy Gaze

Of the Holy One

PEARLS
PRESENCE

Alive as the *Immortal Devotion*

They worship the Light

As The Light

And a thousand hearts who felt alone

Suddenly feel enveloped in the reality of Love

Devotion

Is not something that we "have" to do

Like cleaning out the cluttered garage on Saturday

Or changing the gray sprinkles

Of the kitty box on Tuesday

Or paying a stack of bills on the month's last day

Devotion is something we "get" to do

Like inhaling the pure sultry earthen sacredness

Of the clean sugary fragrance

Of a thousand new dew blossoms

Wafting off a field of forever lilies

PEARLS
PRESENCE

Waving us on toward Home

In the light stream of ten thousand glowing suns

Devotion *then* faithfully moves us

Beyond something we even "get" to do

To that which we *Are*

Devotion cascades up

Like an inverted waterfall

Infinite true life

Welling up and overflowing

As the stable ground of being

Devotion

Riding its chariots of warm golden fire

Delivers you into the womb of enchantment

And births you again and again in majestic redemption

And you shine and shine,

PEARLS
PRESENCE

The whitest of white innocence

And you rest and rest

In the most astounding completion

Valiant Peace Is

Devotion

Is not a duty at religious ceremonies

Or an act performed at set times

Devotion

Is as essential each second

As the air we breathe

Devotion

Is more essential

Than the air we breathe

PEARLS
PRESENCE

A life of no devotion

Is a life of the walking dead

A life that goes faster and faster...

... to... *nowhere*

Devotion is something we "get" to be

As it is something we remember that we "are"

Like feeling the Spirit Wind

Of an eon of celestial Sundays

Breathing You

As the

Breath of Heaven Herself

In the Now of Eternal Tomorrows

Paradise Is

PEARLS
PRESENCE

Devotion

Is not something for a special occasion

Like nibbling a chocolate treat

Nestled with an organic cherry pie

Reminiscing in a rocking chair

Catching up with an old friend

Chattin' 'bout days gone by

Devotion

Is ablaze and afresh

Indivisible Devotion is

Unwilling to be set aside for only a formality

Devotion arises as that which is

Far beyond a familiarity

Yet Devotion deems

Every formality and familiarity

A miracle of the Original *Immovable Love*

PEARLS
PRESENCE

Devotion elevates in luminous vision

As *Adoration's* gold-lined silver wings

Ascendant far above the mundane

Yet the very Light

Of the every single... every single... thing

Devotion

Commands a total surrender

Into the ineffable bliss of

God Alone

As the Beloved of the Heart

The Seat of the Existence

Original Life

The Supreme Devotion:

I Am That

PEARLS
PRESENCE

Remember

Original Creation

Created as the *Immortal Devotion*

That lives forever

As the song of the pure ones

Whose every heart wish

Sprouts a flowered rainbow

Of endless luminous seeds

Blossoming miracle upon miracle

Of the tangible, evident fruits

Of the Tree of Life

These pure wise ones

Mysteriously, mischievously

Shining the secrets

Of the fresh ancient wisdom

Pulse as loyal sapphire fires of knowing

PEARLS
PRESENCE

Alive as the *Immortal Devotion*

They worship the Light

As The Light

And a thousand hearts who felt alone

Suddenly feel enveloped in the reality of Love

"Out of the blue"

How did that happen?

These brazenly practical ones

Softly blaze as the *Immortal Devotion*

And every so called need of life

Overflows with the fruits and flowers

The luminous manna and rivers of peace

Of tangible goodness springing out of "thin air"

For everyone

PEARLS
PRESENCE

How did *that* happen?

Devotion lives the life

And only then the life reflects Glory

Celestial devotion is *The Life*

It endures forever

Immortality's Kindness

Alive as You

Devotion's pillars of honey

Lavishes all these enduring rewards

A puff of devotion this pure

Moves a mountain

A glance of devotion this pure

Raises the dead

PEARLS
PRESENCE

A whisper of devotion this pure

Sling shots flares of pulsing limitlessness,

That light up the skyway with temples of joy

And shower them back down upon the landscape

Like cathedrals of solace, aglow with beauty

If every being lived each breath

Lived each instant

As the Spontaneous Holy Joy,

As Devotion to Oneness with the One God

As the Ineffable Innocence

Of Devotion

Then all beings would spring alive

As a chorus of celestial happiness

All wars and conflicts would end

All hearts would beat in the rhythms of harmony

Like the beat of a billion drummers

PEARLS
PRESENCE

Sounding the soft laughing thunder

Of perfect solidarity,

All voices would sing

Like the tone of a billion serene flutes

Chorusing:

One with the Holy One

Hallelujah

Peace on earth

Peace as earth

Still Home

In God

The Beloved

Selah

PEARLS
PRESENCE

Devotion lives the life

And only then the life reflects Glory

Celestial devotion is *The Life*

It endures forever

Immortality's Kindness

Alive as You

PEARLS
PRESENCE

And they followed that ray of light

All the way back to the sun

And then these holy ones

Followed that Light all the way back

To the Light *before* sun!

And there they found

I Am Light

The Glory of God!

PEARLS PRESENCE

Heaven's Gift of Grace
The Tender Holy Earth Shatterers

Heaven smiles upon us

Nurtures us in bliss

Caresses us in tender love

Answers us in our darkest night

These holy ones

These holy ones

Are One with The Holy One

PEARLS
PRESENCE

These holy ones

Revere and adore God

These holy ones

Have passed through the golden womb

Of the crucifixion-resurrection

Of the ruby diamond Christed pathos

These holy ones

Shatter the earth!

And put it back together

In the essence of Heaven!

Without even moving a nimble finger

These holy ones

Ever being the *Immortal Immovableness*

That is the Endless Love

Of the Infinity of Being Light

PEARLS
PRESENCE

These holy ones

Found a ray of true light

And straightway

Gave up their whole life as a "me"

A "me" that wants this and doesn't want that

And they let all wants hone in

Like a laser beam to One passion:

Home in God Eternal Love: Now

And they followed that ray of light

All the way back to the sun

And then these holy ones

Followed that Light all the way back

To the Light *before* sun!

And there they found

I Am Light

The Glory of God!

PEARLS
PRESENCE

And that light so filled their vision

That one gaze

And the earth scenario shatters

In breathtaking beauty

And a heaven form forms as earth

Visible

Tangible Glory

Hallelujah!

Selah

PEARLS
PRESENCE

The Caressing Rays

Of the Ruby of Ineffable Eternal Love

Washes away all sorrows

As if grievances never dared

To show their shadows

In the face of such immense

And *Tender Love*

PEARLS PRESENCE

Remember the Ruby in the Heart

What if you had a Magical Ruby in your heart?

And what if all you had to do was to know that Magical Ruby
and all suffering ended forever
and all true heart wishes instantly fulfilled, forever?

What if all you had to do was to:

Remember it

Softly fall back and feel it

Unify in it

And trust it

PEARLS
PRESENCE

What if you were only playacting that the Ruby was gone?

And pretending that all this is so hard, or unyielding, or scary

Remember the Ruby

Remember the Ruby

Of course you not only have the Ruby

You are the Ruby

The Caressing Rays

Of the Ruby of Ineffable Eternal Love

Washes away all sorrows

As if grievances never dared

To show their shadows

In the face of such immense

And *Tender Love*

PEARLS
PRESENCE

The Magical Ruby redeems your life

In wonder, grace, beauty

And the majestic grandeur

Of the Absolute

Remember the Ruby

And the miracle of this minute

Will shine garnet starlights of limitlessness

Like waterfalls ever flowing as you

And you will once more live

The true way

You will live as the

Spontaneous Self

In ineffable wings of enchantment

Flying as High Light

PEARLS
PRESENCE

Sashaying effortlessly across the galaxies

Established in trustworthy foundations of

Freedom, and innocence,

Merriment, and luminous creating

God Is

Instantaneous infallible *Love Is*

Live As

The Miraculous Ruby

Of Eternal Love

Free

Selah

PEARLS
PRESENCE

What matters more than
What we go to God for
Is the feeling we go with

Teddy Bear God

I have seen pedigreed persons
Cut down with a flurry of frowns
What they deem a misuse of God

They give the glance of vehemence
To the "sin" of going to God
for "things"

Glaring over bifocals
And shaking their huge heads
With small thoughts,
they gingerly mock and exclaim:
"Santa Clause God!"

PEARLS
PRESENCE

Is God a white bearded figure

That we go to for giggles and goodies?

Or that looks over crimson cheeks

And checks off

If we are more nice than naughty?

Yet, these Dear Ones

The same as us all

Beloved as us all

Miss in that moment

The doorway for sacredness

Far beyond trinkets, toys, and things

Far beyond the ten thousand things

Yes, it's true there's a higher way

Than going to God for things

PEARLS
PRESENCE

In that higher way we know

The Oneness

With and as Beloved God

That deems us miraculously

Fulfilled in all things

Yet, a golden key arises

Far beyond whether or not we

Go to God for things

It's the *love feeling* we have

For most of us

Santa Clause

Was far beyond a thought or figure

Santa: a feeling

The *Santa Feeling* of love and wonderment

PEARLS
PRESENCE

The *Santa Feeling* of excitement and warmth

The *Santa Feeling*

Was like, is like

The *Teddy Bear Feeling*

The key is the Feeling

The deep abiding Feeling

The *Feeling* is the key to *The Relationship*...

...The relationship that builds bonds of love

And castles of the magical, noble forever foundations

That Relationship

Awakens one day

In the glorious luminosity

And sheer holy ecstatic wonderment

Of Oneness

PEARLS
PRESENCE

What matters more than

What we go to God for

Is the feeling we go with

As we feel *The Teddy Bear Feeling*

Innocently dwelling, resting

In the depths of warmth, light and safety

Then we remember Home

And then the deepest

Most sublime realizations

The most astounding eternal truths

Burst our heart alive

With the wisdom of a billion sages

Teddy Bear God

Papa Dios

Father Ahavah

PEARLS
PRESENCE

The child sage

Leads the way

All the way

To the Blinding Light

The Original Light

Selah

PEARLS
PRESENCE

Imagine

You close the golden door

Of this inner sanctuary

And stay inside

Stay inside

Stay... inside...

Until you *only are* the Glory Inside

Until you *only are* the *Holy Heart of Glory*

PEARLS PRESENCE

Glory In The Inner Sanctum

Imagine

There is a golden gateway

A doorway in the front of your heart

A doorway you enter now

Imagine

Your spiritual heart

As One with the Heart of God

PEARLS
PRESENCE

Imagine

This *Holy Heart*

As ineffable immensity of Love

Beyond all space and time

Boundless liberation Heart

Imagine

For now

This *Golden Glory Heart*

Is right here, now

In front of you

Within you

Imagine

You step into,

Yield fully into

This *Holy Heart of Glory*

Right Here

In front of You

As You

Imagine

You close the golden door

Of this inner sanctuary

And stay inside

Stay inside

Stay... inside...

Until you *only are* the Glory Inside

Until you *only are* the *Holy Heart of Glory*

Home Inside

As The Glory

PEARLS
PRESENCE

Feel this

Until it is all you feel

Home Inside

As the Glory

Blaze as this *Holy Heart Temple of Glory*

Feel the Eternal Love

Feel the Living Light

Feel the Holy Joy

Feel the *Quieting*

Feel the Joy-At-Rest we call Peace

If you are one of the rare, rare ones

Who truly will

Truly

Truly

Will

PEARLS PRESENCE

Close the Door

And *Keep it Closed*

Then and only then

Are you the Temple of Light

The true Light of the world

Selah

PEARLS
PRESENCE

Home Inside

As The Glory

Feel this

Until it is all you feel

Home Inside

As the Glory

PEARLS
PRESENCE

If all the past really was,

Was a cry for love

And if all the future really is,

Is a hope the cry for love is answered

Then the answer to the past

And the answer to the future

Is Being *The Timeless Eyes*

To be The Timeless Eyes

Is to be *The Timeless Love*

PEARLS
PRESENCE

Timeless Eyes

Our yesterdays
Are behind us
Or are they?

Our yesterdays
Represent completed scenes
Of a matinee playing
Behind closed doors
Each room with a closed gray door
Signals a segment of time
A time in time

PEARLS
PRESENCE

Our tomorrows

Like a sleeping ember of amber gray

In the distant horizon

Rest pre-dawn

Like latent sunrises unrisen

A time in time

What we call the present

Is only the present

If it is emptied, pristine, clean

Fresh

Otherwise, what we pass off

As the present

Is really the absence

Of You

PEARLS
PRESENCE

When the present is a saturated space

Percolating over with

Thoughts, emotions, sensations

The identities of endless yesterdays

Then a succession of closed, musty doors

Clutters up the open vistas of fresh life

What we pass off for the present

Is really an entrancement with the past

The energetic content of conditioning

Still carried today

Is simply the past in you

Edging out the present,

With focus on the past

These unmet contracted places inside

No matter how subtle

PEARLS PRESENCE

Keep you tethered to the past

And keep you projecting

The present moment

Into the future

The past to future, future to past focus

Veils the miraculousness

It creates a time in time

A time machine

Yet the Reality

You exist as

Is The Timelessness

Stand as Presence

In the zenith of the instantaneity

Of Now

Freshly alive

PEARLS PRESENCE

Beyond all so called "laws" of time

Not bound by past or future or time

The Timeless Self

Exists beyond the time machine

Yet redeems the scenes in the time machine

The Timeless Self

Reveals Itself

Here Now

And the time machine world

Lights up a marquis called: Heaven Now

And the marquis prophesies

The God Reality

That leaps alive across the landscape

Multiplying light rhythms of harmony

Revealing tangible grandeur and beauty

PEARLS
PRESENCE

Be *The Timeless Self*

Spontaneous Adoration

Adoration forms as itself

Adoration's forms spring alive in time

Yet exist as *The Timelessness*

Liberate self from all past focus

Free self from future focus

If you have a vision of new life

Make that vision felt as Now

Ensure that vision

Looks out of the eyes

Of *The Timeless Self*

That sees all as the already finished kingdom

Live as the Ecstatic Presence Moment

Wonderment only lives in the Now

PEARLS
PRESENCE

Know what the Presence Moment is for:

Tender and riveting

Realization of

Timeless Consciousness

The Remembrance of

The Timeless Eyes

Of Immortal Love

Let not a so called past

A foyer of historical screenplays

Keep you glued to the theater chair

Of yesterday's limits

Let not a so called future

Lure you to believe

Some "and"

Exists between you and God

PEARLS
PRESENCE

As if God "and" something else

Can be added in future time

That magically adds to you—

Divine Self Completion

Exists only in

The Timeless Self

The mental-emotional sensory perception

A forgetting of the Presence Moment

A shifting from past to future focus

Fashions a time machine world of make believe

In which a persona protagonist

Stays in the limitation of seeking glory

Rather than Being Glory

Through the thresholds of anointed meekness

The pure ones

Free of past or future focus

PEARLS
PRESENCE

Look out

As *The Timeless Eyes*

Sapphire eyes

Twinkling with the vastness of

Ten million star lit azure skies

The Timeless Eyes

See through the lens

Of Infinity

The Timeless Eyes

Pretend to enter the time machine world

And to get entangled in the matrix

Until Remembrance dawns:

I Am

I Am *The Timeless Eyes*

The Timeless Eyes

PEARLS
PRESENCE

Look out as Light

While seemingly in the dream

Time machine world

Looking out as

The Timeless Eyes

Forever undoes the spell

Of the time machine world

And the time machine world

Collapses into light

And then so instantaneously reforms

As Timeless Paradise

That it seems no gap occurred

Suddenly:

Ineffable beauty and bliss Is

Before all time

PEARLS
PRESENCE

Yet now, The Timeless Vision

Seems to seamlessly reveal itself

In time

Time is an illusion

A temporary flash of sensory perception

Your non-temporary, eternal Timeless Self

Is Reality

Be The Timeless Eyes

Of the Timeless One

One with the One God

Vision Is

The Timeless Eyes

Cast one glance and all yesterdays turn golden

And shimmer as one celestial Now

PEARLS
PRESENCE

One look from *The Timeless Eyes*

And all tomorrows turn silver golden

As One pearl shimmer of luminosity

Of the Eternal Now, Here

Here

If all the past really was,

Was a cry for love

And if all the future really is,

Is a hope the cry for love is answered

Then the answer to the past

And the answer to the future

Is Being *The Timeless Eyes*

To be *The Timeless Eyes*

Is to be *The Timeless Love*

PEARLS
PRESENCE

Vision

Timeless Eyes

Selah

PEARLS
PRESENCE

One look from *The Timeless Eyes*

And all tomorrows turn silver golden

As One pearl shimmer of luminosity

Of the Eternal Now, Here

Here

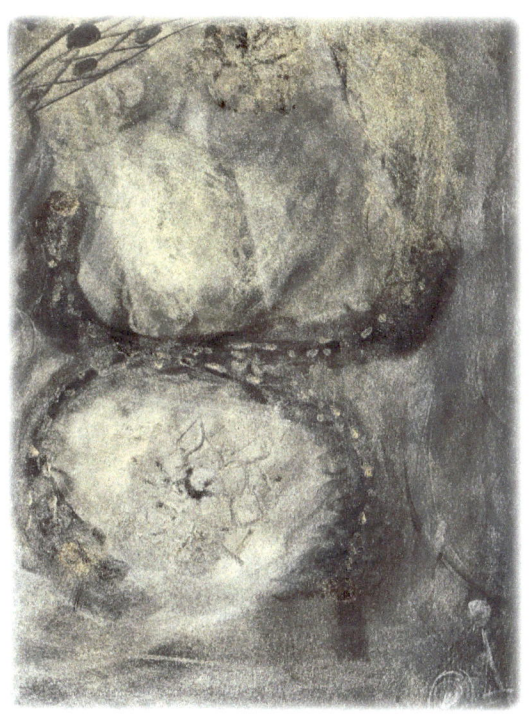

PEARLS
PRESENCE

And *then* the pulsing on

Radiates all the Glory

All the Beauty

All the Immortal Grace

All of the Sacred Bliss

All of the Celestial Flourishing

PEARLS
PRESENCE

The Endless Glory Gap Prior To the On Off Pulse

Eternal

What is Eternal?

Eternal means *permanent*

Eternal means *changeless*

Eternal means *infinite*

PEARLS
PRESENCE

Finite

From "finis"

Means: having an end

Infinite means:

No end

No limit

Limitless

Endless

Life flashes like a cinema movie

And our inner subtle experiences

Of what we perceive

Correlates with streaming finite

Temporary images

We perceive these images

In and as emotions, motions, sensations

PEARLS
PRESENCE

That pulse on and pulse off

The finite movie show
Of so called "inner"
And of so called "outer"
Pulses on and pulses off
In such rapid fire succession
That the pulse on and pulse off
Seems uninterrupted

Consider the Holy Mystery
Of the *Glory Gap*

There exists a luminous *Glory Gap*
Between the pulse on and the pulse off
In that less than a nanosecond,
Instantaneity of a gap

PEARLS
PRESENCE

Only the Eternal Love Is

The Infinite Light Is

Blazing On

Blazing On

That Alone

The only permanence

The only *Real Self*

The only real existence:

Permanent Eternity

Loyally existing in the non pulsing off

Devotedly existing in the non pulsing on

Self

PEARLS
PRESENCE

The warm glow of profound peace arises

As you expand that *Gap*

Rest as that *Gap*

Fall in love with that *Gap*

Come alive as that *Glory Gap*

Be the Awareness Presence

That sees or feels the pulse on

And sees or feels the pulse off

Without identifying as the pulse

Or its finite fabrications

That end and die

And falter and fade

Then you exist as

That Forever Living Awareness

That God Presence

That *Ecstatic Holy Joy*

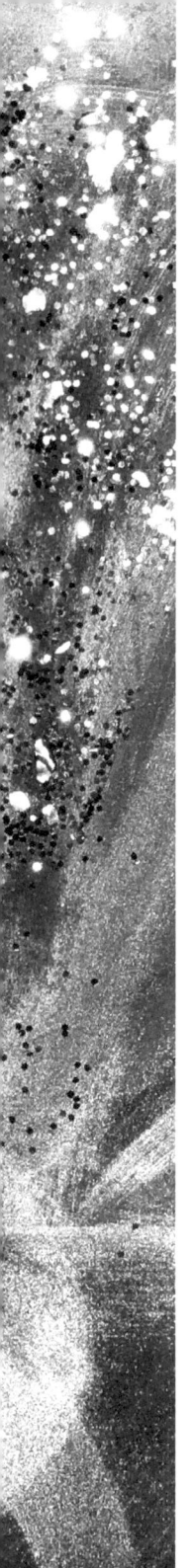

PEARLS
PRESENCE

That *Immensity of Love*

That beholds the pulse

And *then* the pulsing off

Washes away all conditioning

All pain

All suffering

All limitation

And *then* the pulsing on

Radiates all the Glory

All the Beauty

All the Immortal Grace

All of the Sacred Bliss

All of the Celestial Flourishing

Be the *Glory Presence*

Prior to the on, off pulse

PEARLS
PRESENCE

And the pulsing of earth

The pulsing of life

The pulsing of experience…

Will pulse off as the valiant void

That has the wisdom

To release the way things "seem"

Or the familiar way that they have "been"

Or the self that seems separate from Creator

And the pulsing of earth, of life, of experience, of self

… Will seem to pulse on

In the beauty of simple, sacred merriment

And you see

It's the *Glory Gap*

Seamlessly smiling there

The *Eternal Light*

PEARLS
PRESENCE

Prior To

The on off pulse

That now seems to pulse on

And stay on

And stay on

And faithfully stay, stay, stay on

As the kingdom of heaven

The Holy Joy of Paradise

One Light

Eternal

You

Selah

PEARLS
PRESENCE

The Anavah Tender Ones:

Shining in the sanctum of true frivolity

Worshiping in laughing splendor

Flinging genius gifts

From their elegant being

Like an endless infinity of diamonds

The Anavah
Utopia's Free Ones

The key to Utopia

is *The Meekness*

Meek

In Hebrew the word is Anav

The state of being meek is Anavah

Anav:

Meek

To bow down

PEARLS
PRESENCE

To restrain one's power

So as to worship

The One Power of the One God

And express that

In the beauty of holiness

In the mastery of being

The silver lined forever goodness

That casts rainbows of redemption

All over the landscape

Be one of *The Anavah Ones*

Anointed by and in the *Holy One*

Christened in the Messianic Vision

Ordained as the Heart of God

Beating in rhythms of Light

The Heart of Eternal Gold

PEARLS
PRESENCE

The Anavah Ones

Know and intimately breathe

the Primordial Glory of God

They live as *The Ineffable Glory*

In the tender shimmer of the immensity

Of the soft dazzle of the emptiness-meekness

Innocence sings the full chalice of the Hallelujah

Shorn rejoicing surrender

To and As

The Holy One

The Anavah Tender Ones:

Shining in the sanctum of true frivolity

Worshiping in laughing splendor

Flinging genius gifts

From their elegant being

Like an endless infinity of diamonds

PEARLS
PRESENCE

The Anavah Ones:

Gingerly shaking off the crusty chrysalis

Of accretions of repetitive conditioning

Champions in the astute emptying

They bow low and fly high

Spontaneous *Meekness*

Luminous in bliss

Utopia's Free Ones

The Anavah Ones

Leap like fireflies

Dance like olympian angels

His Angels

Sing like celestial crystal tones

Instantaneous *Meekness*

Alight in the Holy Joy

Utopia's Beauties

PEARLS
PRESENCE

The Anavah Ones

Reverence

Sacredness

Still Home in God

In Love with being

The Formless Glory of God

And that Only

That is *The Only*

The Anavah Ones

The Beauty of *The Meekness*

Aware of

The Beauty of *The Meekness*

Alive as the Meekness

The Anavah Ones

Formless Living Light

PEARLS
PRESENCE

Ecstatically complete as *That*

With no need for form to form

Yet all heaven-form forms

For them

As them

The Free

The Meek inherit the earth

The Meek are the vision

That kisses awake

The latent Actuality

Of the kingdom of heaven

And reveals the latent Actuality

As the Reality

The Eternal Love

PEARLS
PRESENCE

And the kingdom of heaven on earth

Springs alive

As if that is all that ever was

That is all that ever was

The Miracle

in a Minute

Of the Eternal Utopia

The Anavah

Selah

PEARLS
PRESENCE

And the kingdom of heaven on earth

Springs alive

As if that is all that ever was

PEARLS
PRESENCE

And, Alas! the Red Sea of the Eternal parts

The pearl gates of immortal happiness

Merrily swing open

The angelic symphony sings on:

A Liberated One!

A Meek One!

Moshe Meek
The Dig to the Immortal Love

Moses

The One Anointed to deliver the people

Moses

The One who stepped forth

And the Red Sea parted

Moses

Did he think he was the greatest on earth?

PEARLS
PRESENCE

Moses

Did he proclaim he had

The biggest mission on earth?

Moses

Did he place his pride in his chosenness

Before loving the one closest to him?

Nay nay

Not the Moshe

Moses, Moshe

Heralded in sacred scripture as

The meekest man on all the earth

PEARLS
PRESENCE

Moses:

Penned in biblical parchment

By holy scribes as-

Meode Anavah

Which means being the state of

exceedingly meek

Imagine when scripture heralds one

The meekest in all the earth

The meek part the Red Sea

The meek inherit the earth

A miracle as great

Or greater

Than the parting of the Red Sea

PEARLS
PRESENCE

Is the parting of one's ego

There is the true liberation

To the promised land

The epic Red Sea parting:

The parting of ones' *positionalities*

The parting of that sharp chard

That would rather wound a heart close to them

Than yield on their rigid hard concepts

The Moshe Meek

Delight and twirl a dervish

To unearth that sharp chard

For it buries deep in the underworld

And forms a golden calf of an idol

PEARLS
PRESENCE

The Anavah

The Meek Ones

Have no idols

They wildly dig for their unyielded places
Exclaiming: "What am I unwilling to give up?!"
Dirt flies everywhere
They dig faster and faster
They cherish finding the idol of unyieldedness
More than all the gold and diamonds of the world
More than all the empires or ministries of the world
There it is!
What a find!

And they see the hidden idol
Buried in the faded robes
Of their unique version of "me"

PEARLS
PRESENCE

Tucked in the familiar personal

Priestly-looking vestments

Defended as for *good causes*

And they see!

The hidden idol-of-limitation

Now looks more like a sack of stones,

And a drag on the heights of the holy ecstasy,

Than the petty salvation substitute

It had been cherished as

The Moshe Meek

Find those resistances

Those things over which

They would rather die

Than give them up

Or would rather lose love

Than give them up

PEARLS
PRESENCE

And they cast them into the sea of woes

With no net to reel it back

Ever

Leave your nets

And, Alas! the Red Sea of the Eternal parts

The pearl gates of immortal happiness

Merrily swing open

The angelic symphony sings on:

A Liberated One!

A Meek One!

Hallelujah!

God Is!

Selah!

PEARLS
PRESENCE

A miracle as great

Or greater

Than the parting of the Red Sea

Is the parting of one's ego

PEARLS
PRESENCE

These *Baby Ones*

These soft true leaders

Brandish a razor sharp clarity and maturity

They wield the God Authority

In true surrender, devotion and *Grace*

Leadership: The Baby Ones

The wayshowers of the world

The anointed leaders of this epic hour

Will not govern

With feet swiftly moving to craftiness

Or heavy hands executing domination

Rather than controlled hearts

And tough skins

The real leaders

Have unconditioned hearts

Radiant kind skins

PEARLS
PRESENCE

And the laser beam

Unborn vision of nascent Light

The real leaders

Have Baby Eyes

The Soft Blaze that Knows

The Holy Gaze

The Unborn-yet-born Way

Looks out as Love

The *Baby Ones*

Brain wave state

Is open and sensitive

Rather than spouting repetitive trained thoughts

So blindly fond of hearing themselves

PEARLS PRESENCE

Talk and talk and talk,

The *Baby Ones*, the Humble Ones

The Emptied, *Listening Ones*

Hear and Voice

Divine impulses

Of fresh vibrant genius

These *Baby Ones*

These soft true leaders

Brandish a razor sharp clarity and maturity

They wield the God Authority

In true surrender, devotion and *Grace*

They govern with a power

Born only of the purity of God

PEARLS
PRESENCE

Be one of the *Baby Ones*

The Baby...

Unborn all the way to the Original Light...

An anonymous adult saint on earth

The *True Leaders*

Just in time....

Selah

PEARLS
PRESENCE

You walk on ice

And you exclaim:

This is the highest bliss!

This is paradise!

You walk on ice

And you see

You *know*

That when you "need it"

The ice melts just long enough

To walk on the water

Of any situation

As the miracle

Walk on Ice

We think of spiritual life in so many ways

We think of walking with God in so many ways

We say:

We walk hand in hand with God

We say:

We walk on solid ground with God

We say:

We can depend on God

(though most do not *really* believe this)

PEARLS
PRESENCE

We say:

Bless your heart, God loves you, relax Dearie

We say:

God helps us

We even say:

The Bible says "God helps those that help themselves"

(Though that is written nowhere in the Bible)

A time comes wherein the cotton candy

Of these placating sayings—

That a friend says while they lightly touch our hand

And toss in a sympathetic nod,

Or that *we say* in the corner of our minds

Where we bubble wrap our denied aversions

A time comes when these sayings,

That pepper and punctuate coffee shop chatter

That serve up superficial crumbs of comfort

No longer stimulate

No longer comfort

No longer inspire

Then we see that our comforts and dependencies

Our habits and attachments

Casually banish us to the sparse outer courts

Far from the cornucopia chalice

Of true divine intimacy

That offers the inner sanctum

Of our only genuine *Happiness*

The Gem of Genuine Happiness

We harvest only in the *True Intimacy*

The lived reality of Oneness with the One God

PEARLS PRESENCE

Which means Oneness

With the Beloved God, as *Love*

The Immortal Love, the Ineffable Love

Stands at the gate

The Glory Presence: ready to open the gate for you

If only you have the key to the lock

Only one key exists

No locksmith out there can fashion it for you

It comes from the heart

Inside you

The passageway key into *True Holy Love...*

Is...

Total trust

PEARLS
PRESENCE

When you go all the way

All the way to the core diamond of Love

All the way to the ecstatic joy of adoration

All the way

Home in God, the Holy One

All the way

To the Holy Joy

Of Immortal Life

All the way

To Glory

To Limitlessness

You sign up to walk on ice

You walk on ice

With no hand to hold

You are upheld with *The Heart*

That holds You

PEARLS
PRESENCE

You walk on ice

That seems so slippery

You stop trying to reach for a hand rail

You ascend in the Heart

So high

That Trust walks as You

Trust breathes You

Second by second

Trust stabilizes You

You walk on ice

And you exclaim:

This is the highest bliss!

This is paradise!

You walk on ice

And you see

PEARLS
PRESENCE

You *know*

That when you "need it"

The ice melts just long enough

To walk on the water

Of any situation

As the miracle

You walk on ice

And you see

You *know*

That when you "need it"

The ice turns into diamonds

And you blaze as a diamond light

Singing celestial symphonies

Of Blazing Glory

Of Tender Joys

PEARLS
PRESENCE

You walk on ice

Knowing you cannot look back to the past

You will hit a hole in the ice

You cannot look to the future

You will slip forward toward falling

You rejoice to be free of past and future focus

That you may feel... all... the... Love...

All the Love

Only fully felt

By abiding as Presence Moment

Here Now

Go for the gold

Run for the ice

And stay there

It's the warmest place

It's the highest space

It's the wonderland of Christmas

Every morning

It's the deliverer of true rest

Every evening

Hallelujah

Fly free

By loving the ice

By Loving the Giver of the Ice

Giving the Ice

Is Giving The Divine Love

The Divine gives It's Self

To You

PEARLS
PRESENCE

Silence Is

Trust

God Alone

Intimate Beloved Love

Trust it alone

And ride the chriots of the rubies of Love

On the ice

All the way *Home*

Selah

PEARLS
PRESENCE

Sometimes

Oftentimes

Mosttimes

Only three words are needed:

I

Love

You

Three Words

Words, words, words, words

Notice when you feel you need
To speak lots and lots of words

Ten thousand words
For the ten thousand thoughts
Of the ten thousand opinions

Watch the words, words, words

Have you said ten thousand
When *three*
Are needed?

PEARLS
PRESENCE

Three words

Three miraculous words

The words that make no words needed

Sometimes

Oftentimes

Mosttimes

Only three words are needed:

I

Love

You

Selah

Home in the Heart Foundation

A Chartered, 501(C)3 Tax Deductible Charitable Foundation

Prolific Free Teachings, Books, Audio Messages, Online Book Library

Global Outreach, Training/Elevation of Spiritual and World Leaders
(Online and at Retreat Center, Florida US.)

Global Classroom and Sacred Land Centers for In-Person Interactives

Forums for Grace: The Direct Experience of Deific Love

Addressing the Core Cause of Suffering: Perceived separation
From God, to live as Eternal Love, The Light of Consciousness

Melting Divisive Judgments, Revealing the Unifying Principle and Presence
In families, religions, teachings and "paths"

Restoring the True Heart of Christ Teachings, Presence, Consciousness

Opening Direct Experience of the Underlying Deific Love & Wisdom
At the core mystical-sacred-essential heart of all Paths

Home in the Heart Foundation, offers free teachings, books, messages that offer guidance, support and wisdom in the direct experience of Oneness with and as God Presence. The Foundation focuses on the liberation from suffering by addressing the core root of humanity's unresolved issues of separation, pain, and instability.

The teachings and creative offerings support the direct Face to Face, Heart to Heart, Consciousness to Consciousness awakening in the Reality of God Presence, Deific Love, as the true Origin and ground of being, happening each instant.

The ministerial outreach restores the lost meanings and direct Oneness teachings of mystical (sacred) Christianity, the original lost teachings of Christ, supporting the clear living of Christ Presence-Consciousness. The Foundation messages weave the core heart wisdom teachings and realizations of the most high, pure teachings of the core religious distinctions. The Foundation bridges/melts the superficial divisive layers of religious divisions, revealing One Heart, One Family, already present in the deepest truths of each path.

Whether The Absolute Supreme Creator Presence is known and experienced as Mother Father God, Yahweh, Mother Mary, The Light, Consciousness, Brahman, Adonai, Elohim, Bhagavan, Pure Land—the way opens now for the One Original Light, the One Eternal Love to be experienced as the ground of being….lived, lived here now as heaven as earth.

...e Foundation supports the remembrance of Home, as an instant by instant experience of Primordial Love, of the vast Light of ...nsciousness, honing the freedom from identification as a personal self into crystal clear focus.

Home in the Heart Foundation

Holds the Vision of Sacred Land Centers,
Offering Space for Spiritual Community Gathering

And Global Outreach To Millions of Beings,
In support of Direct Spiritual Realization

Of Deific Love
And Unifying Wisdom-Peace

We welcome you to the Mother Ahavah and Home in the Heart Foundation Family

Pearls of the Presence: Heaven's Way on Earth is more than a book. It is a simple, sacred, and miraculous way of life. It is one of many treasures offered as part of a ministry, serving a global audience.

Mother Ahavah and Home in the Heart Foundation is devoted to the remembrance of being still Home in Eternal Love, and living that in tangible, practical daily experience.

The message, materials and outreach support all beings in living as authentic happiness and peace.

We invite you to share this book with others, and to be blessed with our other literary and creative works by Ahavah, Dr. Ann Marie Nielsen:

Free Morning Messages, Free Online Book Library, Gift Audios, Music Samples
Books, Classes, Class Programs, Canticle Songs,
Contemplative Prayers with Musical Accompaniment,
Discourse Programs, Paintings, Photography, and more.

motherahavah.com

THE GROUNDBREAKING BOOK BY ANN MARIE NIELSEN PH.D

Father Ahavah:
The Unfathered Ones Come Home to Love

Ahavah: a word for Love in the Hebrew language and scripture. Father: Father Spirit, Eternal Father. Thus, Father Ahavah means the direct experience of Everlasting Father God Love.

Father Ahavah is a way of life and a pathway of light. Our hearts, relationships, emotions, health, prosperity— and our environmental and world conditions—have been tragically impacted by the longing for fatherly love, wisdom, and protection. This message reveals the longing we share for the Father's Love. Ultimately, this Father must go beyond a human person, or gender; it must go beyond an object, or something seen as external or personal. This Father Ahavah is known as Eternal, as the One God, yet felt as a gentle Papa, as a present, compassionate Father. And yet this Father Spirit, this Father Heart, this Father God Light is within us—is us, as us.

Father Ahavah bears similarity to Somewhere Over the Rainbow. The song speaks of and carries the lower tones of the aching, the longing that we share. Then the song hits the high note, rises to the rainbow, and over the rainbow, way up high. The vignette "true story" sections of the Chapters reveal the low note, the en masse longing, the sense of separation. And the Now Wisdom Teachings and the Experiential Applications portions of the chapters hit the high "C," the high notes, the celestial tone, and takes us to the Holy Joy.

However, in the Wizard of Oz, the real world happens in Kansas. In this book the real world is the golden world of Light. More specifically, the real world reflects ineffable Divine Love in the kingdom inside. And yet that world of Light is lived here, now, from the heart in the most relevant, tangible, practical way.

Review by U.S. Congressman, Bill Johnson

"Making people, regardless of who they are or where they are from, aware of the depth, strength, and power of their spiritual self is a tremendously powerful life changing, therapeutic tool. Father Ahavah does that, and it will open the door for a return to The Heart of the Father for millions of people. It is not, however, an easy read. Not because of the writing style, but because of the spiritual depths that Dr. Nielsen's words take the reader to. It takes time to let the words really sink in. The only writings I have read that come close to accomplishing the same thing is the Bible."

– U.S. Congressman, Bill Johnson
Ohio Sixth District

Father Ahavah is available at Amazon and all good book stores worldwide.

You Hold Me — the Canticle album from Ahavah (Dr. Ann Marie Nielsen)

Ranging all the way from soft acappella tones, to epic instrumental orchestration with four part cathedral harmonies, this ascendant way of merging voice, tone and melody, offers you a deeply moving and elevating heart experience.

The Canticle songs immerse you in the felt remembrance of sacredness, peace, and Eternal Love in a way that liberation's awareness remains with you.

The Canticles originated as spontaneous songs of worship that Ahavah, Dr. Nielsen sang and toned through the course her day — whether nestled in her prayer room, contemplating beneath the grandmother oak trees by the water, holding a retreat gathering, performing ministry activities of her Home in the Heart Foundation.

She had no plan to professionally record and distribute these tonings of stillness and grace—initially seen as offering silent blessings to the world in quiet moments, secretly and sacredly sang to heal and awaken hearts throughout our humankind family. In the recorded audios, Ahavah sings the lead vocals, background vocals, four part harmonies and she tap dances the percussion.

Ahavah, *You Hold Me* album

In the words of Ahavah, "I clearly remember an intuitive flash as a child, that sound would one day emerge as a primary and powerful way to feel God's Presence. I had no idea at that time or until quite recently, that sound and song would arise as such an intimate and sacred expression of my voice in the world."

The ineffable joy and love of God Presence, Face to Face is indescribable. I feel this experience pulsing through as melody and tones, which I usually initially tone without words for some time. Then spontaneously one day, lyrics arise. I entrust the hearing of these songs to you, that you rest in the Glory of our Creator, the beauty of your sacred heart."

Listen to free samples of the *You Hold Me* album:

motherahavah.com

About Ahavah
Dr. Ann Marie Nielsen

Ahavah, Dr. Ann Marie Nielsen, author, spiritual teacher, founder and President of Home In The Heart Foundation, Inc.

As a young child, Ahavah (Ann Marie Nielsen) began having spontaneous, holy encounters, feeling the intimate Presence of God. These experiences of Deific Love, later increased in depth and frequency, over decades of contemplation, meditation, and direct experience.

Today, Ahavah embodies and presents the Mother Ahavah spiritual teachings and retreats — guiding in silence, wisdom, authenticity, meditations, practices — supporting the stable direct experience of intimacy with the Divine. This awakening as Deific Love unifies all paths in the core oneness: Aliveness as Divine Love, as Original Light, as the Infinity of Consciousness. The teachings wed Love and Wisdom, guiding in the realization of Self as Original God Presence, this instant, as the true ground of identity.

Ahavah offers prolific creative sharing, original teachings that melt the core matrix of suffering and limitation. She offers these teachings via international live classes, retreats, books, canticle songs, and art.

Her vision includes the individual and global awakening in Deific Love, the realization of the Original Light of God in/as all beings, the dissolving of division among couples, families, groups, religions, countries, and spiritual teachings.

Ahavah centers teachings and meditation on embodiment: the tangible lived experience of direct God Oneness. She lives, holds retreats, writes, paints, sings canticles and ministers in Florida, United States. Her books, articles, classes have reached persons in 109 countries.

www.ingramcontent.com/pod-product-compliance
Lightning Source LLC
Chambersburg PA
CBHW041513220426
43668CB00002B/11